Joseph's Dreamcoat

and other stories

Text by Juliet David
Illustrations by Elina Ellis
Copyright © 2019 ZipAddress Limited

Published by
Lion Hudson Limited
Wilkinson House, Jordan Hill Business Park,
Banbury Road, Oxford OX2 8DR, England
www.lionhudson.com
ISBN 978 1 78128 356 1

First edition 2019

A catalogue record for this book is available from the British Library

Printed and bound in China, August 2019, LH54

Joseph's Dreamcoat
and other stories

BY JULIET DAVID
ILLUSTRATED BY ELINA ELLIS

CANDLE
BOOKS

Joseph the dreamer

Jacob had twelve sons.

He loved every one of them. But he loved Joseph more than all the others.

One day Jacob gave Joseph a beautiful coat.

This made his brothers feel very jealous. Joseph always got the best presents!

Sometimes Joseph had strange dreams.

"I dreamt we were in the harvest fields," Joseph told his brothers once. "We all had bundles of grain. But your bundles bowed down to mine."

Joseph's brothers were very angry.

"Do you think *we* should all bow down to *you*?" asked one brother.

The brothers' plot

"Your brothers have led the sheep to new fields,"
Jacob said to Joseph one day. "Take some food for them."

So off he went.

When Joseph's brothers saw him coming, they said,
"Here comes our brother, the dreamer. Let's get rid of him!"

Just then, some men rode by on camels.

"Let's sell Joseph to these traders,"
said the brothers.

So the traders carried Joseph
off to the land of Egypt.

Joseph in jail

The traders took Joseph to a market.

Soon a rich man called Potiphar bought Joseph to be his slave.

Joseph worked hard for Potiphar.

But one day Potiphar's wife told lies about Joseph.

She said he had treated her badly.

Potiphar believed his wife, and threw Joseph into jail.

Poor Joseph!

But God had a plan for him.

Strange dreams

One night Pharaoh, king of Egypt, had strange dreams.

He told his dreams to his wise men.

He wanted to find out what his dreams meant.

But the wise men had no idea!

Then one of the king's servants said,

"I was in prison – and a man called Joseph explained my dream."

"Send for him at once," ordered Pharaoh.

13

Joseph helps the king

The king of Egypt told Joseph his strange dream.

In his dream, the king had seen seven big, fat cows.

Then seven skinny cows had come and swallowed the fat cows.

Joseph explained the king's dream.

"For seven years," said Joseph, "there will be great harvests. But there will follow seven years with *no* rain and *no* food in your land."

When the king of Egypt heard this, he put Joseph in charge of gathering grain, to feed his people during the hungry years.

Joseph's family now all came to live in Egypt. They were called "Israelites".

A baby in a basket

Long after Joseph died, another king made the Israelites work as slaves.

"There are just *too many* Israelites," he said angrily. "Throw every Israelite baby boy into the river!"

One Israelite mother had a beautiful baby.

She was afraid the king's soldiers might snatch him away.

"Let's make a basket of rushes," she said to her daughter one day.
Then they floated the basket in the river.
The princess of Egypt came to the river to bathe.
She saw the baby in the basket – and loved him.
She called him Moses, and took him to the palace to live with her.
God kept baby Moses safe.

God speaks to Moses

When he grew up, Moses ran away to live in the desert.
There he became a shepherd.

One day, while Moses was looking after his sheep,
he noticed something strange.

A bush in the desert was on fire – and it just kept burning!
Moses went closer to look.

All of a sudden a voice spoke from the fire.

"Come no closer!" It was God speaking!
"You're on holy ground."

Moses was frightened!

"Go back to Egypt," God said to Moses.
"Tell the king of Egypt to let my people go."
"I can't do that," said Moses.
But God promised to help him.

19

Moses meets the king

Moses went to the king of Egypt's palace.
"God says, 'Let my people go!'"
he told the king.

"I don't know your God," said the king. "Why should I obey him?"

Instead the king just made the Israelites work even harder.

Because of this, many terrible things happened to the Egyptians. Each time something bad happened, Pharaoh said the Israelites could leave.

Then afterwards, he changed his mind.
Finally one night the oldest Egyptian boys
all died.
But none of God's people died.

At last the king said to Moses, "Go – leave Egypt!
Take your people and go."
God's people were free at last!

The sea dries up

Now God's people left Egypt and marched into the desert.
    But the king of Egypt changed his mind yet again.
    He sent his army to chase after the Israelites and bring them back.
    Meanwhile Moses' people had reached the shores of the Red Sea.
    But they had no way to cross the sea.
    God said to Moses, "Hold up your wooden stick!"

Moses did as God told him – and the waters parted.
Moses led his people on a dry path across the sea.
Then the waters fell back. The Egyptian soldiers could not follow.
God helped Moses save his people.

Joshua captures Jericho

When Moses had died God gave the Israelites a new leader.
His name was Joshua.

Joshua marched his army to the great city of Jericho.

He wanted to capture this city – but it had high stone walls
and heavy wooden gates.

"March around the walls of Jericho for six days," God told Joshua.
"On the seventh day march around the city seven times.
Then blow your trumpets and shout as loud as you can!"

The Israelites did just as God told them – and the seventh time
on the seventh day, the city walls collapsed.

God gave Joshua the great city of Jericho.

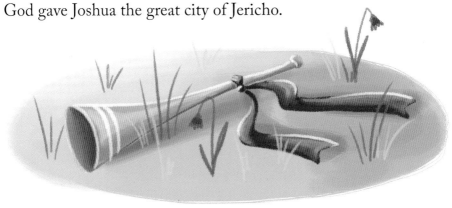

God answers a prayer

An Israelite woman named Hannah went to God's holy tent.

"Lord, give me a son," Hannah begged.
"When he grows up, I'll give him back to help in the holy tent."

Eli, the chief priest, was watching.

"Go home, Hannah!" said Eli. "God has listened to you."

Hannah felt sure she was going to have the baby son she wanted so badly.

And she did.

"We'll call our little boy Samuel," she said when her baby arrived.
"And I'll give him to help in the holy tent, just as I promised."

Samuel listens

Hannah kept her word.

When Samuel was old enough, she took him to Eli, the high priest.

"I've brought Samuel to help you," she said.

One night, while Samuel was asleep, he heard a voice call, "Samuel, Samuel!"

He thought it was Eli and ran to the old man.

"Here I am, Eli!" he said. "You called me!"

"I didn't call, Samuel," said Eli. "Go back to bed and lie down."

The same thing happened three times.

At last Eli realized it must be God calling Samuel.

"If you hear this voice again," Eli told Samuel, "say, 'Speak, Lord – I am listening.'"

Samuel went back to his room.
Soon the voice came again, "Samuel! Samuel!"
This time he answered, "Speak, Lord – I am listening!"
And God did speak to Samuel.
He told Samuel he would be a leader of Israel.

David defeats a giant

A huge giant called Goliath was bullying God's people.

No one was brave enough to fight him.

But David, who was just a shepherd boy, said,
"I will fight this giant!"

The giant laughed when he saw little David.

David had *no* sword and *no* spear. He had only his shepherd's sling.

David chose a stone – *whizz* – it flew through the air. The stone hit the giant on the head, and he fell to the ground.

God helped young David beat the giant Goliath.

A temple for God

King Solomon built a wonderful temple, where the Israelites could pray to God.

The builders used huge stones to make the Temple walls and fine wood covered in gold for the furniture.

The ark of the covenant, which contained the stones with the Ten Commandments on them, would be kept in the Temple.

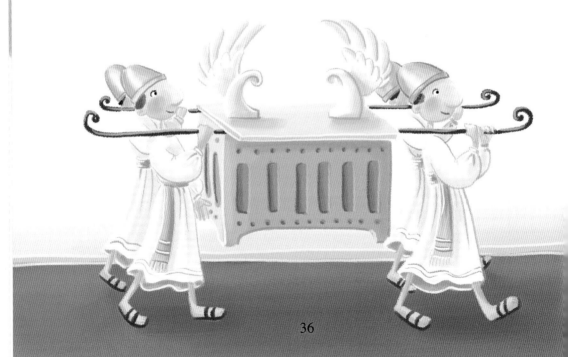

When the Temple was finished, Solomon held a special service.
Priests carried the ark of the covenant inside.
The Temple was filled with dazzling light, to show
God was with his people.

Esther saves her people

Esther was a Jewish woman. She was married to the great king of Persia.
One day she heard a man called Haman making a plot.
"I want to kill all Queen Esther's people, the Jews," said Haman.
Esther was frightened for her people, so she made a plan.
She invited Haman and the king of Persia to a banquet.

At dinner Esther told the king, "Haman is plotting to kill my people."
The king was very angry. He arrested Haman.
Esther was brave. She saved her people.

Saved from lions!

Daniel was a good man. He prayed to God three times every day.

One day the king made a new law: "No one may pray to God. If they do, they will be thrown to hungry lions."

But Daniel kept praying to God, three times *every* day.

Some men saw Daniel praying to God. They told the king.

The king was sad, because he liked Daniel.

But not even the king could change the law of the land.

So soldiers threw Daniel into a den of hungry lions.

Daniel prayed to God to help him – and an angel shut the lions'
mouths.

God kept Daniel safe from the hungry lions.

Rescued by a fish

"Go to the great city of Nineveh!" God told Jonah. "Tell the people there they must stop doing bad things."

But Jonah *didn't* go to Nineveh. He ran away instead.

Jonah sailed off in a boat going the other way!

Suddenly a fierce storm blew.

Jonah said, "God sent this storm to punish me."

So the sailors flung him into the sea to save themselves. Jonah thought he was going to drown.

Down into the swirling water he sank.

Then, *gulp*! Something swallowed Jonah.

He found himself in the tummy of a great fish.

God left him there for three days and nights.

At last the huge fish spat Jonah out on the seashore.
God saved Jonah from drowning.
"Go to Nineveh!" said God again.
This time Jonah didn't argue.
He jumped up and went *straight* off to Nineveh.

Other titles in the series